A New Thought Journey through the 12 Steps

A New Thought Journey through the 12 Steps

KAREN LINSLEY, MA

Balboa Press books may be ordered through booksellers or by contacting:

Balboa Press
A Division of Hay House
1663 Liberty Drive
Bloomington, IN 47403
www.balboapress.com
1 (877) 407-4847

Print information available on the last page.

ISBN: 978-1-5043-3171-5 (sc)
ISBN: 978-1-5043-3172-2 (e)

Balboa Press rev. date: 5/1/2015

Dedication

There is no one person who I can say thank you to, no one person who passed on to me what I needed to know to function somewhat normally in life, and to ultimately write this book. So I dedicate this book to the legions of people in recovery who have gone before me, and made life possible for people like me. And I specifically dedicate this book to my teachers. Roberta, who has always been there for me, no matter what. Sue, whose rich discussions have allowed me to know there is always a different way of learning. And many other men and women who have taught me the meaning of unconditional love and acceptance. I also dedicate this book to Nikki Campbell, without whom I would have been unable, and perhaps unwilling, to attend ministerial school. And to my mom, Norma Linsley, who taught me that there are two sides to the concept of lack and limitation. To my dad, the Rev. Dr. Gil Linsley, who gave me the Three Magic Words, and to my step-mom, the Rev. Dr. Gail Linsley, who outlasted them all.

Preface

I'd like to begin with a thanks. Thank you for being here, thank you for participating in your journey and all the richness and fullness that life has to offer, and thank you for buying and reading this book!

Next I'd like to say a few words about New Thought and the 12 Steps.

New Thought, at least as I am using it, refers to a movement mainly represented by Centers for Spiritual Living[1], although there are other organizations which are also considered New Thought. The term itself refers to new ways of thinking about ancient wisdom, wisdom such as that written about by our ancestors in books such as the Bible, the Koran, the Torah, the Bagavad Gita, and passed on orally by our Native American and Buddhist ancestors. We teach in New Thought that such works were never meant to be interpreted literally, but instead metaphorically. We rely on science, psychology and philosophy to correctly interpret this literature, and also on the writings of founder Ernest Holmes. While not discounting New Age, I wish to make a distinction between the two: New Thought is not New Age, although we do attract many New Age people to our centers.

---

1 www.csl.org

Now about the 12 steps. I realize I am going to encounter some controversy by daring to interpret….rewrite if you will…the 12 steps. We interpret everything else in New Thought, why not this? And, from my personal experience, I have discovered that translating the original 12 steps into more modern language is a more inclusive way to go about things. The original language quite frankly turns many away. I'd like to see the power and beauty and joy that results from taking the 12 steps, in all people who wish it. What I have written here is not AA, nor is it any other 12 step program. I would absolutely be against any person, meeting or group taking what I've written here and calling it AA, or any other program that ends in the word "Anonymous." That would not only violate the traditions which keep AA and other 12 step groups alive, but it would not serve AA, nor would it serve anything else. And, if you do have an addiction that is at the critical stages (what they call stage 4 in treatment lingo), I HIGHLY recommend taking the steps as they were originally written. Do that first, then revisit this book.

As to my qualifications for writing this book, I am a very proud minister in Centers for Spiritual Living, currently serving a pulpit in Carson City, Nevada. And because I honor the traditions of AA and other 12 step programs, I will simply say that I have 28 years of rich and full and beautiful recovery from alcoholism and drug addiction, and I wouldn't have it any other way. In this 28 years, and especially more recently, I've encountered many people who want a change in their lives, but simply cannot get past the original wording of the 12 steps. So this is for you dear reader. There are no accidents in life, and if you are reading this, you are meant to be reading it. Use it, work it, and watch your life change for the better.

Introduction

Did you ever wonder how some people seem to sail through life with dignity and grace, and some, well....not so much? Did you ever wonder how some seem to be floating on a cloud of peace and light, and some move from one drama du jour to the next?

Did you ever wonder how those pillars of peace did that?

Well, it is possible for you to be a pillar of peace!

How? How, you ask, can it be possible to be a pillar of peace when I'm losing my house, I've lost my job, my partner left me, I've been diagnosed with a life threatening illness, I've got a tiny little addiction issue, or I just can't seem to get ahead in life?

It is not only possible, it is probable. Yes, there is some work involved. But it isn't the kind of work you would think. The work is on the inside. We'll leave the outside stuff be for now. All that stuff: the lost job, the wayward partner, the illness.....that's the outside stuff, and it's going to do what it is going to do. You are going to be peaceful, no matter what, if you do the things suggested in this book.

I'd just like to add a little something here: yes, I'm promising peace, no matter what. But that doesn't mean you aren't going to feel loss, sadness, anger or pain. It doesn't mean you get to bypass your grief work. It just means you are going to feel ok in the midst of the loss. It just means you are going to feel ok even if you are angry or sad.

The world is full of paradoxes, and this is one of them. How is it possible to feel ok when the sky is falling? It's because there is an inner and an outer. What we think, our values, and our beliefs are our inner world, and our outer world is what we call the world of effects: the stuff, the events, the circumstances, the conditions. This book isn't really about changing the world of effects, although that will be the ultimate end result if you do the things suggested here. This book is about changing your inner world.

There are so many schools of thought that teach the same thing: change your inner world and your outer world will change. Take your pick: spirituality, religion, psychology, philosophy. They all have a version of the same truth: the inner effects the outer.

Since this book is not about justifying that basic truth, but about showing you how you can take advantage of it, I'm not going to go into the evidence. If you choose, you can research it yourself.

This book is organized into 12 chapters. Why 12? Why not 11...or 13? I happen to think that the number 12 is a big deal. There are 12 months in a year, 12 jurors in a jury, 12 years of basic schooling. The Greeks had 12 Olympians and 12 labors. The Hindus have 12 main gods. Christianity has 12 disciples, 12 apostles and 12 stars. Two sets of 12 in a day. And worldwide, literally millions of people live happy lives today because of a thing called the 12 Steps.

And I'd like to say a word here about the 12 steps. This book is my rendition of the 12 steps. It is a synthesis of everything I have learned in almost 30 years of studying and applying the 12 steps in my life. These steps are powerful beyond words. They contain the wisdom of the ages, but because of the traditional and sometimes religious language in which they are written, some people experience blocks. I'm not here to espouse the old party line of "if the language drives you away the misery will drive you back." I'm here to say there is a way through, simply by changing the language a bit. I've taken my experience and knowledge of the 12 step programs, and my training and experience in New Thought, and simply changed the language. I hope this will help you, dear reader, experience all the gifts that they have to offer.

I wish to emphasize that this is not AA, nor any other 12 step program. I also wish to emphasize that while I believe anyone can use these steps to improve their life, if you are experiencing acute addiction, I invite you to either join a 12 step group or get professional help, using all the tools available, before approaching this in the way I've suggested it. This book is really more for people who have moved a bit beyond the more acute stages of addiction.

If you do the work suggested in this book, I guarantee your life will change, and I guarantee it will change for the better. I highly recommend that you utilize the services of a guide, mentor, emotionally healthy friend or coach for this work. Trying to do this alone is the hard way.

Chapter 1

1. We admitted we were ready for a change in our lives.

What's with the "we?"

You may notice the words "we" and "our" in this first statement. I've chosen to use those words for a very powerful reason: this isn't something you need to do alone. I happen to believe that this is very definitely something you should not do alone. There is help. Coaches, guides, mentors, good friends are all available to assist in this inner work. I've designed this book so that you should be able to navigate the levels on your own, but I highly encourage you to share your journey with someone. It will make traveling the road much easier.

How can you tell if you are ready for a change?

Do you find yourself saying things like: "something has to give, I can't go on like this anymore!"? Or perhaps, "this can't be happening!" Or perhaps you simply feel a vague sort of dissatisfaction with life in general? Or maybe something disastrous has happened. The reason doesn't matter. I will go out on a limb here and say that if you are reading this book, it is no accident. You are ready for a change. Finding books like this, and thinking that life would be better if... means that you have a call. It doesn't really matter where the call came from, or even why. What matters is that you honor that call. There are no accidents in life. If you don't heed the call now, I would happily bet that you will receive a much louder and less gentle call in the near future. A life threatening illness, or a break up of a relationship, or a loss of job are all calls….it isn't about the loss (although, again, doing the grief work is essential), it's about the opportunities inherent in the loss.

This first level speaks to a quality of life that sucks. It speaks to a loneliness, a feeling of separation from our fellow humans and from Spirit. If your life sucks, if you have answered affirmatively to the questions above and said, "Yes, I am ready for change, I want change, and I'm willing to proceed based on that desire," then you have completed the first step!

It is as simple as that. Simply setting an intention, or making a commitment to proceed, is all that is needed here. All that is needed is willingness. In being willing and setting an intention, you set in motion a series of powerhouse events. Get ready, because it is likely that from this point on you will indeed begin to experience some monumental change. Both inner and outer. This is another reason why it is good to have your support staff in place, so you can keep them apprised of the changes occurring in your life.

I want to say a word here about the temptation you might have to write about this. To write about why you want change, or why you are at this place in your life, or what happened to get you here. Resist that temptation. Please. This isn't rocket science and the more you attempt to complicate it the more difficult it will be. Consider that an attempt to complicate this by writing about why is more of the same. You've acknowledged that you want to change. Start now and resist the temptation to go into your history of why. This first step isn't about the story. It's about moving forward. Don't look back now. Focus on the forward.

Focus on your intention. What you focus on expands, and if you focus on the story, on what happened previously, you will get more of the same. Focus forward. If you want change in your life, simply move forward with the next step.

Chapter 2

2. Became willing to change our thinking, both about ourselves and about the role of spirit in our lives.

Now that we've admitted we are ready for a change, it is time to look at where change really happens. We are trained, especially in western society, to believe in the world of effects. In other words, we are trained to place more importance on what we look like than what we feel like, more importance on how much stuff we have rather than how we feel about that stuff, and we are trained to get what we can get when we can get it, through just about any means available, and let everyone else worry about themselves. We are also trained to think that the more we do the more we are worth, and that "exhaustion is a status symbol."[2] We live, as Mary Morrissey[3] likes to say, in a condition based world. Placing emphasis on outside appearances and stuff is the way we've been trained, at least in western culture. And we are trained to think that God is a separate entity, existing somewhere outside of and separate from ourselves.

Our training has sucked.

---

2 Brené Brown, Daring Greatly

3 Mary Manin Morrissey, http://www.marymorrissey.com/

It has not served us, on any level. It has created an entire society of people have ignored their inner callings to do and accomplish what the world told them they must, and it has created generations of people who are constantly striving for that greener grass on the other side, never realizing they have forgotten to tend their own grass in the striving. It has created a segment of people who would rather spend two hours writing a complaint letter about $2 worth of merchandise, because they would rather win than anything else. It has created a society of lonely, alienated humans who don't think they matter in life. It has created a populace of professional victims, who think they can't control anything in their life because God is sitting up there somewhere pulling all the strings. When something bad happens they ask why God did it to them and when something good happens they don't claim any part in that good because God did it all. It has created a population of people who say there simply isn't a God, there can't be, because none of that religious stuff makes any sense. And it has created another segment of folks that say, there might be a God but I'm really disillusioned with him because look at all this bad stuff that has happened to me and to others. It has created people who think God does stuff, and that God has our backs. And many of those people who believe that are now either disappointed and alienated from God, or they think they aren't worthy of all the good stuff that God does. Our training has contributed significantly to living fear based lives filled with judgment, intolerance, hatred and violence.

I have good news: we can be untrained. And we don't have to live that way. This is the promise that this process offers. Change your thinking, and your life truly will change.

We can change the way we think. In fact, we must change the way we think, or we will be doomed to more of the same old same old.

And right here is where we reach a major hurdle, and it is where many people stop cold in their tracks. Because part of our training says that this can't be changed. We've been threatened, cajoled, manipulated and told we would go to hell if we didn't think a certain way. So when we begin to consider changing that thinking, all of our self-preservation instincts waken with a loud protest of "OH NO WE AREN'T DOING THAT!" Some people call this the ego. It is the ego's job to protect us and it feels very threatened by change.

Here is where you remind yourself that you began this journey because you wanted a change in your life. Again, change comes from within. You can try an experiment and see if it works: try and change something outside of yourself without changing your thinking. Get involved in a new relationship, or get out of an old one. Change jobs. Move. Notice what happens. Nothing changed, except now you have added grief for the loss and chaos for whatever change you did. You took yourself with you. Where the change needs to happen is within ourselves, not out there.

I first came across this quote many years ago. A friend of mine got it from his therapist. He did not believe the quote, and as a result is still mired in misery, asking over and over again, "Why has God done this to me?" He refused to believe that he could change his life by changing his thinking. Here is the quote, variously attributed to Anonymous, transcendentalist Ralph Waldo Emerson, Chinese philosopher Lao Tzu, supermarket magnate Frank Outlaw, spiritual teacher Gautama Buddha, and the father of Margaret Thatcher:

"Watch your thoughts, they become words;
watch your words, they become actions;
watch your actions, they become habits;
watch your habits, they become character;
watch your character, for it becomes your destiny."

If you are doubting that your thoughts have power, and that simply by changing your thinking you can change your life, consider that this quote is attributed not just to many different people, but that those people represent many different paths. How can so many paths be wrong? This quote is simply another way of stating a truth: what we think and believe is what we receive.

If you are having trouble believing this basic truth, then this is another of those times when your support group can be very helpful. Use them. Tell them what you are trying to do. Voice your fears and challenges, talk about stuff. Don't keep it in, no matter what. You are only as sick as your secrets. Unload those fears, voice them to someone who won't try and fix you, but will simply listen with a compassionate ear, then move on.

Just be willing to move on, and consider that you've tried everything else, and you are still experiencing the same old same old, and that you set an intention to do this process.

The first step to changing your thinking is to be aware of it. It is very helpful to find a way of recording your thoughts at this stage of the game. A handwritten journal works well for some, but you can also use the note feature in your phone. Take a few moments at key times during your day to ask yourself these questions: what is the overall trend of my thinking right now? Ask yourself if there are certain times of the day when you feel more positive than others? Times when you feel more negative than others? Where does your thinking automatically go when, for example, someone tailgates you? What do you automatically think when someone pays you a compliment?

Once you begin to get a sense of your thoughts and the overall pattern of your thoughts, it should be pretty clear as to which thoughts are serving you and which aren't. For example, if someone pays you a compliment and you either don't believe them or you come up with an excuse for why it is not true or no big deal, that is very good information to have about yourself. Does it serve you to not believe it when someone pays you a compliment? How? Does that kind of thinking perhaps need to be changed?

And, once we are aware of which thoughts serve us and which don't, we can begin the sometimes arduous process of changing the ones that don't serve us. This takes more awareness, and consistent and continuous reminders to ourselves that we are at choice in our thinking, and we can think differently. This will not happen automatically at first. Like many other behaviors in life, thinking is a habit, and it takes conscious effort at first to change a habit.

It is also an excellent idea to be cognizant of how you wish to think instead. For example, instead of pooh poohing a compliment, what would serve you better? A sincere thank you and an inner sense of gratitude that what the person said was true? Perhaps an inner acknowledgment that you did good? An inner pat on the back? Maybe some exploration as to why you don't believe it is in order. Or maybe simply a willingness to believe that what the compliment giver said was true.

Many times changes in our thinking will come only as a result of willingness. Willingness is a great beginning.

As you become aware of the patterns of your thinking, you can also be making notes about what you would like to think instead. Consider making two lists, side by side. One list is titled: here is how I now think. The other is titled: here is how I wish to think.

Here is where the support staff can come in handy. You may want to consider giving them a copy of your lists. That way they can remind you when you automatically fall into old patterns of thinking. And you will. Don't let it discourage you. Just continue to gently bring your thoughts back to where you wish them to be.

Now, what about this spirit stuff?

Part of this level says that we are willing to change the way we think about the role of spirit in our lives.

You may have been brought up with a more traditional view of God: outside, separate, male and only speaks to us through intermediaries such as priests. God is in charge, God does things, God has our back. And you can only find God on sacred ground, such as the church.

Or you may have been brought up as I was: I'm the product of an atheist mother and a New Thought father. To say I was confused is putting it mildly. My father told me my thoughts had power, and that God was within me, and I was a part of God. My mother told me if I wanted anything done I had to do it myself because I couldn't rely on anyone for anything, including God, because he didn't exist. What resulted was an independent young lady who relied only on the god within and never asked anyone for anything, including god.[4] And for many years I ignored that god within, choosing instead to concentrate on the world of effects. When the world of effects didn't go my way, I drank, used drugs and men, and basically blamed the world for my problems. It was a pretty lonely place to be.

You might be an atheist. You believe in science. "Show me the proof!" You can find the proof in quantum physics. I do not claim to be a scientific expert. In fact, science is my weak spot. But I know enough about quantum physics to know that what New Thought teaches is true: our thoughts effect our conditions.

4 When I capitalize God, it means I am referring to the more traditional God. When I don't capitalize it, it means I am referring to the god within us.

Consider that everything is energy until our thoughts collapse it into physical form, which is quantum physics. And also check into the Observer Effect, which states that the outcome of any experiment is effected by the thoughts of the person conducting the experiment.

My point here is twofold: there is nothing wrong with what you believe, if it works for you. What is this spiritual stuff for anyway? Isn't life all about being happy and at peace? Isn't life all about being comfortable in our own skin? If you are happy and at peace and comfortable in your own skin, then your beliefs are working for you. If you aren't happy and at peace and comfortable in your own skin, then it is time to change your beliefs. Unless of course you think life is something to survive and then you die…in which case I would ask you why you are reading this book.

Here's a concept to think about: We are here to express and be as physical manifestations of god. God has no way to experience the physical except through us. This is what "in the image and likeness of God" means in the Bible. What matters is how we feel about ourselves, and how we live, move and have our being in the world. That's what matters. Just like you can change your thoughts, you can also change how you feel and what you believe about God. There is a reason there are so many books and teachings about God. Many don't call it God, but it's all god. You don't have to call it God, or even god. Call it whatever you want. Just remember that thinking of god as something separate from you is likely to continue more of the same: a feeling of separation, which will carry over to all of your affairs. You will feel separate from other people, from good, from nature, from everything, if you begin with feeling separate from god. Begin with oneness, and you will feel at one with everything else. Separation is where loneliness lives. Oneness rids us of loneliness.

I also understand that while many people say they believe in the concept of oneness, that god is within, they still persist in thinking of god as something outside and separate from themselves. That's ok, if it works for you. But ask yourself if it is really working.

Part of this journey asks that you find something spiritual that affirms your strength and power and provides you will comfort. If you choose to call that something science because you believe in the laws of science, then go for it. As long as it makes you happy.

I once worked with a lady who labeled herself as atheist. She wanted happiness, she wanted freedom, and on some level she knew this process was the way to get it. We worked together and she came up with a belief that worked for her. It was ok for her to use science as her god. It was ok for her to base her thinking on what science could prove or disprove. I keep in touch with her, today she is happy, fulfilled in her life, and free.

I once worked with another person, a guy who knew on some level that all the talk about a God separate from him was not what he believed, and didn't serve him well. He isn't the only one who has come to the conclusion that god is Love. Love works for him, and is providing a freedom and a peace and a happiness that allows him to experience life on a grander scale than he ever dreamed of.

My point here is that it simply does not matter what other people think God is. What matters is what you think it is. Turn your attention away from what society thinks, what others think and what you've been taught or trained to think, and go within and find a concept that works for you.

About 18 years ago, I had a sudden shift in my concept of god that has become the foundation for what I believe today, and it serves me very well. Outer conditions in my world back then were not good. I had just gone through a divorce, and I was devastated, and couldn't get off the couch. I knew, somehow, that trying to change the outside wasn't going to work. I had ten years of recovery under my belt and I knew that the answers lay in a deeper exploration of what god meant to me and how it worked in my life. I dove within in a quest to deepen the connection and expand the understanding I already had with a god of my understanding. The book "Conversations with God," by Neale Donald Walsh somehow found me. I don't even remember now how that happened. But I remember reading that god wanted for me what I wanted for me and something inside me clicked. It all came together with my New Thought roots, and my understanding of god moved from something separate and outside of myself and not really effective, to inside and powerful and gentle and loving and kind. I began taking classes at my local Center for Spiritual Living to explore that. Every class I took facilitated an inner change, which then affected an outer change in my life. Today, as a minister in that same organization, I get to continue my personal journey and teach the concepts to others.

I'd like to say a bit about the difference between religion and spirituality here. When I speak of spirituality, I mean compassion, connection, an acknowledgment that there is some force, some Thing that connects us all and makes us part of the one. Call it love if you wish, embodied in and through each of us. This something is not about rules or dogma, but about feelings and peace and joy and beauty. Religion is something different. Religion is Christianity, Judaism, Islam, or Baha'i. There is nothing wrong with religion. If it gives you comfort and power and strength so that you can live a happier life, great. But if it simply feeds the doubt and fear within you, if it makes you feel lonelier and more alienated, then find a new god or a new religion.

God is big enough to be what you need it to be, no matter what. Here are a few secrets about god that may (or not) surprise you: god doesn't do things. God simply is. God doesn't care, not really. It wants for us what we want for us. We have free will for a reason. All that stuff about being created in its image? It's because we were: we are the physical embodiment of god. We are not all that god is, but we are part of it. To deny your godself is to deny a huge chunk of you, and that is the reason you feel unfulfilled, unhappy and lonely. I take it a step further and claim that god can't experience the physical except through us, so wouldn't it be like honoring god to live the most highest expression of our godselves that we can?

These are my personal beliefs about god but they stem from what I learned taking classes in New Thought, which is taught at Centers for Spiritual Living all over the world. They don't need to be your beliefs. Your beliefs are yours and you have a right to them. If they serve you well, keep them. If not, change them. I'm not asking you to believe what I believe. This isn't about religious control of people, this is about giving you tools so you can live a happier life. I'm asking you to find a belief system that works for you.

Here are some ways to discover a god that works for you:

Ask yourself: What does god look like, feel like, sound like? Where does it live? How do I access it? If you are a visual person, you may wish to draw a picture. My first god was Group of Drunks. No, I'm not talking about drunk people on the street. I'm talking about sober alcoholics. Those people were sober and happy, and I wanted that. They became my god for quite some time until I was able to find a god of my own that worked for me. My second God was the process of working the steps. That process gave me a new way to think. It changed my personality at a deep level (which, by the way, is the definition of a spiritual awakening). And guess what? That god still changes. It's like a work of art: it is a living, moving, breathing work in progress. God is big enough to handle that, it is the me that keeps changing, so my concept of god keeps changing.

At this stage of the game, you need not worry about end results. The point is to be willing, to simply open a door. You don't need to step through the door, nor do you need to know what is on the other side. Just be willing to change your thinking, about yourself and about god. Be willing to consider that your thinking may not be serving you. It probably did at one time. It might not any longer, and this is a good sign that it is time to change it. This is an ongoing process that won't stop.

Chapter 3

3. Became willing to expand my concept of spirit, so that I feel connected to it and safe with it.

More god stuff. Yep. Whatever you have conceived of to this point, make it bigger. Larger. More powerful.

God is such a wonderful thing. It doesn't care what we think about it, whether we turn our will over to it, or what we call it. What this level really does is set us up for the next levels, where we will be digging a bit. We need something to turn to when we dig in the muck of our lives. We need it for strength and upliftment when discouragement and fear set in. Change is effected from the inside out, and the next several levels are a road map for going within, a place that is very dangerous territory for many. So with this third level, we need something that will allow us to enter that territory knowing we are safe.... no matter what.

What makes us feel safe? What makes you feel safe? What makes you know without a doubt that all is well, no matter what the conditions may be? For me, it is Love. God as love, love as god, love love love. Love from my fellow humans to me, love from me to them. It is also nature. I spend a lot of time outdoors. I can't look at the sky or witness a sunset or feel the energy of the little hill I climb every day without also thinking of god. And it is oneness. Knowing that I am one with the most powerful entity in the known universe alleviates all loneliness and worthlessness and lack.

It is that Thing, that Force, that Isness, that allows me to move within and know that no matter how dangerous the neighborhood is inside my head, I am safe.

Get a concept of a god that works for you, and then move on, remembering that concept is like a work of art, constantly changing.

So in this step, we continue to change our thinking, to explore bold new worlds, and figure out what god means to us. And again, it isn't rocket science and total comprehension isn't needed to proceed. Just a willingness. Here is where a mentor/guide/whatever you want to call it comes in real handy. When the thinking goes back to the old way of being distorted by fear, the mentor brings it back to love if you are unable to do so yourself. Yes, expect that you will need some help here with reminders that you are engaged on a new way of thinking and being. The way we think is habitual, and like any other habit, changing it is going to take conscious effort at first.

You may want to read some books here; I've listed many authors in the appendix that I have found helpful. Some of them have written many books, some just one, do some research and see if one or more of these authors calls to you. You may want to explore and play a bit here, but don't do so at the expense of continuing on this journey you have committed to. You can continue to explore while you continue your journey.

Chapter 4

4. Made a series of lists designed to allow us to get to know the most important person in our lives: Self.

This level is about using lists to keep things simple, to keep us from diving so deep into our story that we can never get out, and to facilitate a journey into peace and freedom. Lists are wonderful things. When you lay them all out and expose them to the light of day, all sorts of patterns begin to emerge. It is these patterns that we will be looking at in order to change the way we think and believe.

The first list is a list of your fears. What are you afraid of? Things that go bump in the night? The IRS? The Big C? Being alone? Spiders? Falling off a horse? Dogs? Cats? The gremlins under the bed? List them all. With each one on the list, list what you do when you encounter the fear. Do you kill the spider? Or do you run away? When you go off your horse, do you walk away from the horse, resolving never to ride again, or do you get right back on? Do you blame the horse, or do you look at your position when you went off, with an eye towards what needed to be corrected? What do you do when you are in fear? Flight or fight? Or perhaps freeze? Or some combination, depending on the circumstances? This list is quite possibly the most valuable one you can make because it will give you key bits of information about yourself. What you do with a little fear is the same thing you will do with a big fear, only magnified. Learn to recognize when you are in fear, and you are well on your way towards freedom from fear, which is what this entire process is all about.

I believe (not everyone does) that there are only two basic states of being. Fear or love. And I believe that those two states can't coexist together in the same entity. In other words, you are either coming from a place of fear, or you are coming from a place of love. You can tell very easily which it is: if you are coming from a place of fear there is likely to be anger, attacking, blaming, shaming, attempts at manipulation and/or control. Or you may be one of those that simply shuts down in fear: can't feel anything, can't act. Or you may run away. Find out how you react to fear, so that you can recognize it when it happens. Fear is not something to be denied, but it is something that we can use to keep ourselves out of trouble.

Love, on the other hand, feels wonderful. Coming from a place of love allows us to be compassionate with ourselves and others, it allows us to be confident, it allows us to take responsibility, it allows us to be fully present for our lives. When coming from a place of love, we are likely to experience the warm fuzzies. When coming from a place of love, chances are we can communicate kindly and gently, we can show up for what is, and we aren't trying to control the people and the world around us. Love has a tendency to solve problems that are unsolvable.

Your fears list will be very educational. Again, list what you are afraid of, and how you react when you encounter it.

Set this list aside for now, and begin with a clean sheet of paper. By the way, sometimes, when making these lists, it will all come out at once, like a purging. Allow that to happen if necessary, but also allow for a more gradual process. It may be that you simply place two or three items on your list each day until you are done.

It doesn't really matter how you do it, but be consistent. The one thing you don't want to do is sit on this. Making this list is like digging up mud in a pond. When it is muddy, you can't see clearly, and it isn't very pleasant. Sit on the list and your pond will stay murky, causing you no small amount of discomfort. You will get covered in gunk. If you need to, make a commitment to add at least three items to your list every day.

The second list is actually a column, the first of 4, of people, places or institutions. It should run up and down on the left side of your page, with about 4 lines in between each item on the list. What determines if someone or something should be on your list? Basically, if it comes to mind for whatever reason, it goes on the list. Some common items are ex-partners, law enforcement, government, bureaucracy, parents, siblings, other family members, teachers, authority figures, the weather, Democrats, Republicans, Christians, non-Christians....I think you get the idea. If you think of it, it isn't a done deal in your life, even if you think it was. You wouldn't be thinking about it if it was done. Add it to the list. Don't question it. It won't hurt, quite possibly will help. And don't second guess it. Just make the list, and move on. And don't exclude the positive things. That teacher that made all the difference in the world when you were a kid. That random act of kindness from the guy in front of you at the Starbucks who paid for your coffee. Again, if you think of it, it should go on the list.

You will know you are done making the list when you run out of things to put on it. Only you can say how long this list will be. Don't try to predict it, don't try to explain it, just make the list, not forgetting to leave 4 lines in between each item.

Draw horizontal lines in between each item on your list. Draw vertical lines down the page, so you have a series of boxes about two inches square. The items in that second list make the first column of boxes. You should have three additional columns, each with a series of boxes running down the page.

It will look like this:

People, Places, Institutions that have had an effect on your life	Why are they on the list?	What was threatened? How did I feel? Feelings based on fear here.	How did I react to that? (usually with dishonesty, manipulation, blame)

Take as many pages as you need, but be sure to only allow about 4 lines in each box. Again, it isn't so much about the story here, but about getting this stuff out in a format where you can take a good look at it and notice the patterns, because this is where the solution will lie. If you really feel a need to tell your story in detail, hire a psychologist to listen to you. Such detail in this process will only bog you down.

Your third list (the second column on this particular sheet of paper) will contain the answer to the question: why are they on your list? Basically, what happened? We aren't looking for a biography here, just the basics. You only have a two inch square for each item. If your mom made your list, why? Did she ignore you? Beat you? Smother you? Die on you? If your ex made the list, why? Was he/she unfaithful? Did he/she abuse you? If the teacher who made all the difference in the world made the list, why? Did she show you that learning was a wonderful way to escape? Or perhaps she facilitated learning in such a way that you got it? Or maybe she recognized a talent in you that no one else had, and encourage it. Why did the Starbucks guy make the list? Did it perhaps show you a different way to be? Or maybe it just brightened your day?

Once you complete this part, you will have a beginning, and some patterns should be emerging for you.

With the third column on this list, we turn our attention and thoughts away from THEM. In fact, we need never revisit THEM again. You are done with THEM. This is a key turning point in this work. THEM is the story, and while the story won't change, your view of it is going to. If you want to be free. If you don't, stop right here and continue living life as you have lived it up till now.

When I began my studies at CSL to become a Practitioner, and then a Minister, they told us that the story is basically unimportant and irrelevant. This is another of those things for which we've had a lifetime of conditioning and training. Generations of psychologists and therapists have spent years listening to us dig into our stories. In doing so, we've concentrated more on our stories than on what we wish to be and live. We have placed our energies and our thoughts on our stories, and created more of the same, because that is where our focus has been. I will remind you that what you focus on expands, and you can either focus on the story, on THEM, or you can move on. Moving forward from this point you will find complete freedom, moving backwards will simply keep you stuck.

Keeping your attention focused on THEM from this point forward means you are choosing to keep your attention on the problem, not the solution. It means you are denying yourself the biggest and best gift you have to offer, the gift of freedom from fear. Moving your attention away from them and onto yourself means you have made major progress towards being a pillar of peace.

This is where so many people get stuck. I urge you to continue the journey.

I have a personal story to share about how powerful this process is. It is the same story I mentioned before, where I found Conversations with God. Here are a few more details: I was 42 years old, ten years sober. I was about six months out from a divorce, and in serious trouble. I couldn't get up off the couch. I was sleeping pretty much round the clock, I couldn't work, I wasn't eating properly, I certainly wasn't getting any exercise, and I wasn't letting my support group know about it. That divorce devastated me. Forget about the fact that a basic value for me is that marriage is a lifetime commitment. Forget about the fact that I absolutely was wild crazy in love with my ex. Forget about the fact that I was very lonely in that marriage because as I grew into a place where intimacy became more acceptable to me, he didn't. As I asked for more intimacy, he withdrew more and more. I had met him when I was a year sober. He was less than 24 hours sober. No, it wasn't a healthy thing for me to do, and I certainly don't get involved on that level with people new in sobriety anymore. But back then I was still pretty unhealthy myself, and all I knew was that I was in love, quite possibly for the first time in my life. We married a year after we met, and I thought I had completed my life's mission. I was sober and loving it, I had a career I loved, and I had my husband. Eight years later he wants out. I was a lonely neglected young lady, and anger became my state of being. Especially after he told me, on his way out the door, that he had never loved me. He said he had married me because he knew he would stay sober if he was with me. That one statement literally took me to my knees, and I believed it and allowed it to become the foundation of a basic feeling of unworthiness.

I felt like my entire marriage had been a lie. I felt betrayed, worthless and totally and completely powerless. Anger gave me a sense of power. It was a false sense, but I did not know that at the time. I ranted and raved and accused our common friends, who were kindly honoring both our journeys, of taking his side. I became a very unpleasant human being. I joined a softball team, and hit that ball far using my anger and pretending the ball was him. I voiced his wrongness and my rightness to anyone who stood still long enough to let me get the words out. I hung out in that anger, because it was the only way I knew to have any control whatsoever over my life. And then the depression hit.

I knew, intellectually, that anger makes us sick. But I was unwilling to let go of that anger because it was the only way I felt like I had any power in my life at all. Forget about God, forget about everything else. I held onto that anger like a life preserver. Until I realized I was in jeopardy of losing my business because I couldn't go to work. And I realized I was in jeopardy of losing my health, both physically and mentally. I picked up the phone and called my mentor, who told me to get my ass to the doctor. I went. I got some help. And I did this process. I put that man on my list, and I listed what he had done to me. And then I had to make the last two columns. I had to turn my attention away from him and towards myself. He may have victimized me originally, but he was gone. I was now victimizing myself and I was doing a pretty good job of it. If I wanted to heal, I needed to live in the solution by looking at my part, not his.

When I did that, when I turned my attention away from him and towards me, it was like a big weight lifted off my shoulders. It happens like that sometimes. One day I was angry and miserable and living in fear and hating life, the next day the sun was shining, I felt light and carefree. I was able to resume my life, happily going back to work. The biggest gift of all was that I was truly able to wish him well. We ended up being friends, and I was able to sincerely call him "loving ex-husband" when I referred to him, and mean it.

People who haven't done this process don't realize the power of it.

So what is in those almost magical third and fourth columns? What happens there to allow us to move from victim to empowerment? What happens there to allow us to take responsibility for our lives, and step out in love, instead of living in fear? A simple shift, from looking at THEM and what they did to us, to looking at us and how we felt and reacted, makes all the difference in the world.

I want to say a word about shame here. For most of us, and I was no different, looking at ourselves means shame. We look at our ways of thinking, our behavior and we hang our heads in shame and guilt. UGH. NO! That is not what this is about. We think the way we have thought because we were trained to do so, and we behave the way we did because it was the only way we knew to survive at the time. We may have to pay some consequences for our behavior, but being ashamed or guilty or a bad person and living in that and focusing on that will only create more of the same. Remember that what we focus on expands. Focusing on shame or guilt or thinking we are basically bad or unworthy will only result in us being more ashamed, more guilty, and feeling more like we don't deserve anything good. This is a key area where changing our thinking is essential. Going back and looking at our thoughts and feelings and behavior is not about shaming ourselves. It is about taking a clear look at what is serving us and what isn't. We get rid of what is not serving us, and replace that with what will serve.

Here is a perfect illustration: In many classes and workshops at Centers for Spiritual Living, you will be advised to clean the clutter. Clean out the closets, clean out the wallet, clean out the cupboards and shelves. There is a spiritual principle behind this which is key, and comes into play in doing the work at this level. The new cannot come into our lives until we let go of the old. It is as simple as that. Most of us don't shame ourselves when cleaning out a cupboard of stuff we no longer use. We may have used it at one time, but we don't any longer. Why then, when cleaning our minds and emotions of things we no longer use, do we insist on shaming ourselves? Do not shame yourself. Please. It isn't productive, and it will prevent you from moving forward and experiencing all the joy that life has to offer you. Just take a look at the clutter, clean out what you no longer use with gratitude for how it did, at one time serve you, and move on.

If you are ready to make a major, permanent, powerful change in your life, you will proceed.

The third column asks us to review how the event or person on the list affected us. Did it threaten our sex life, our financial life? Did it harm our sense of security and safety in the world? Did our pride get damaged? Did it harm our self-esteem? How did you feel when it happened, and what were the resulting thoughts?

Again, don't get stuck here. Yes, they did wrong. Yes, they hurt you. Staying stuck here will keep you in the hurt. Those people who did you wrong most likely don't even think of you or the incident much. They are going about their lives. You staying stuck here means you are only victimizing yourself, over and over again.

This third column is a transition column of sorts. With this column we are shifting our attention from THEM to ourselves. Here we begin to see some patterns. Perhaps every item on the list damaged our self-esteem. Or perhaps every item on the list made us feel less and less safe in the world.

Also consider that fear is prevalent here. It is the common thread in all the items. Remember your fears list, and how you react to fear, because that is key to the next column.

The fourth column asks us what our part is. This isn't an opportunity to cynically say that I shouldn't have gotten in the relationship in the first place, then it would not have happened. You can go there if you want, but in doing so you will stop this process dead in the water. This is the time when we look at our behavior. We looked at our feelings in the third column. Now we look at our reactions (as opposed to our well thought out responses). Did we lie or cheat? Did we not communicate honestly and openly? Did we run away? Did we manipulate so we would get our own way? There are some words for this: dishonesty, selfishness, self-centeredness. Again, this isn't about shame. This is about looking at what kinds of behavior does not serve us, so that we can let it go and replace it with something new.

Your patterns might become fairly obvious here. You might take a look at this and realize that you always ran. Or you always tried to control or manipulate. Or you always had a backup significant other waiting in the wings so that when the current one didn't work out you had another waiting.

When you sincerely look at your part, you will realize that you did some things that didn't serve you well, nor did they serve others. I cannot emphasize the importance of having a support system in place for this part. There will be grieving. All the stages of it: denial, anger, bargaining, depression and acceptance. (see Elizabeth Kubler Ross[5] for more on this). It is normal and

---

5 http://www.ekrfoundation.org/

healthy to go through these stages. Suppressing them with drugs will make them worse. Jumping into a new relationship immediately to cover up the feelings of loss of the old one will simply guarantee that the new relationship will fail.

Tough words, yes. But this is important. It is important to allow yourself to feel. It isn't pleasant, and no one is claiming that it will be. But you don't need to prolong the unpleasantness by being ashamed. Feel the grief. Those stages will happen in no particular order, and as in any other grieving process, you will likely find yourself in tears at the most inconvenient moments. Allow it if you can. Express anger in appropriate ways. Allow yourself to rest and be quiet. If depression reaches a stage where it is clinical, get professional help. And acknowledge with gratitude the acceptance when it comes.

Chapter 5

5. Share what you have discovered.

Pick someone in your hopefully-by-now-well-established-support-network to hear what you've discovered. Their job is to listen with compassion, and also to lovingly point out any patterns that you may have missed.

This isn't about sharing a biography of our lives. Remember, the story is done and we don't return to it any more. We are sharing how we felt when stuff happened, and how we reacted when we felt that. We are sharing how our behavior got us into trouble.

Remember you are only as sick as your secrets. And remember that the person who is listening to you has likely experienced and done something similar.

Many people feel very vulnerable doing this for the first time. This is normal. And consider that vulnerability is like a magic key, unlocking the door behind which lies joy and beauty and all the richness life has to offer. Don't mistake that feeling of vulnerability for distrust. Distrust is merely another roadblock we create for ourselves to justify not doing the process. Don't go there. If you are feeling distrust, either pick another to share with, or recognize that the distrust you feel is more about your opinion of yourself than whether or not the person with whom you are sharing is trustworthy. This isn't about them, but about you. This isn't about feeling comfortable either, it is about unloading some key pieces of stuff that no longer works, so you can load up on stuff that does work. You are sharing feelings and behavior. They are listening, not judging. Confidentiality is a big deal, of course. Don't share this with a gossip. Don't share this with someone who is only ever able to talk about others and not themselves. Wisely select the person with whom you choose to share. And don't allow old feelings of distrust prevent you from moving forward.

Once you've finished the process of sharing, you are likely to feel tired. Go home and take a nap, or go for a walk. Spend some time in the quiet with yourself. You've done a huge incredible thing here. Acknowledge that. Cry if you need to. Sleep if you need to. It is about self-care at this time. It may occur to you that you forgot to share something. If so, call your selected listener up and share that. Give yourself a little bit of time to rest, and contemplate this new way of life that will now emerge with the next levels.

Chapter 6

6. Be ready to enlarge our connection with spirit, using that connection to realize we can let go of that which does not serve and replace it with that which does serve.

This level is about beginning to think in terms of what we want to replace that old stuff with.

We've begun the process of changing our thinking. Now is the time to consider what we want to change it to. From fear to love. From blame to responsibility. From lack to abundance. From limitation to living life full on!

More god stuff here. We are now aware, perhaps more fully aware than we've ever been before. It is important to remember not to go into shame, but simply to be aware of thoughts and behaviors which do not serve us. And to ask for help in changing those. We continue to enlarge our concept of and our connection with spirit, whatever that is for us. This isn't very mysterious. We take action, and we ask for help in ways that work for us. For me, asking an outside God to change my thinking and behavior doesn't cut it. Acknowledging that the god within me wouldn't think or act that way, and enlisting the support of my network, and consciously changing one thought and action at a time is what works. Now that we are aware of our thoughts and actions which don't serve us, we can begin to change them. It won't happen overnight, but it will happen.

This level is more about being ready than about actually doing the work. You really need not spend a lot of time here. Remember the analogy about clearing the cupboards? This is the level where you've looked at what is there, and decided what you want to remove. You haven't actually removed it yet.

This level is about saying goodbye, with gratitude, to those things which likely served you well at one time but no longer do.

I recommend making another list here. Can you tell I like lists? I think they simplify things, and here you can simply things a bit. Remember the list in step 2, of the ways you no longer wish to think, and the ways you would like to think? You can use that list here, or make a new one, and use it as a basis to form some affirmations about yourself that you can feel. Putting feeling behind the written words packs a powerhouse punch that can't be denied.

Chapter 7

7. Continue the process with a request.

This is the level where we actually remove the items from the cupboards.

This is about asking for help. We've hopefully already learned to do that. We ask for help and willingness to change our thoughts and our actions. We ask for help from that spirit within, or whatever our understanding of that is. And we ask for help from our support staff. This level is about continuing the process begun in step 2: actively replacing the old thinking with new ways of thinking. Remember, your thoughts create your destiny. Now is the time to use that list you created and modified, and to focus on the new ways of thinking.

Levels 6 and 7 are simultaneously simple and very very deep. For example, I believe that we always get what we ask for. The key here is that it doesn't really work like that. It works that we get what we ask FROM. If we ask for good and abundance in our lives but are still hanging on to a belief that we are worthless, we will continue to manifest examples of worthlessness. If we ask for abundance, we must believe and think that we are worthy of abundance. We don't get what we ask for, we get what we believe. This is an ancient truth that is restated over and over again in all the religious and spiritual literature. Even the Observer Effect in quantum physics says that the belief of the experimenter affects the outcome of the experiment! So it doesn't really matter whether your god is spirit or science, this works the same way. And changing our beliefs about ourselves is really what these two levels are all about. They aren't about changing our actions. That's a result. You can't change your actions consistently and expect to be able to keep it up unless you also have changed beliefs and thinking. Change the thinking and the beliefs and the changed actions will happen normally and naturally.

Ernest Holmes tells us that not only must we change our thinking, but we must keep it changed. I think our list can be a powerful tool here, because during those times when discouragement or despair or negative thinking sets in, we can turn to the list and actively and consciously turn our thoughts from the ICK to the positive stuff.

Chapter 8

8. Made a list of all persons we had harmed, and became willing to make amends to them all.

I've taken the wording directly from the steps of AA here. It is a powerful step. We will need to revisit some of those people in that first column in level 4. The ones where, in the 4th column, we did something to them. We may have stolen, or been dishonest in our communication, or lied to them. By the way, this doesn't make us a thief or a liar. It simply means we did that behavior at one time. I am not a fan of calling oneself names, especially names like liar and cheat. I believe in the power of this process, and in the power of a god of my understanding, to change who and what I am. I call it my being. I've had discussions with people who simply do not believe that such a fundamental change can happen in a human being. They think that if they lied and cheated before in their lives, it makes them a liar and a cheat for all time. My ex-husband was one of those. And the reason I speak of him in the past tense is because he is dead now. He died of an overdose and was found on floor of his slum apartment. A charismatic, witty, smart man who manifested money and abundance wherever he went, is dead because he refused to believe that his basic character could not change.

There is a definition of a spiritual awakening in the AA textbook[6]. It says that a spiritual awakening is a personality change, or a "profound alteration in our reaction to life." This is what this process promises. You can change your character, but the beliefs you hold about yourself need to change as well.

Here we are only making the list, we aren't doing anything yet. There are two schools of thought in the making of this list, and I don't know that it really matters which one you subscribe to. One school says that we use our first column that we made in step 4 as our list. The other says we make a new list. Both have merit. There are likely some people on the first column that won't need an amends. Don't get bogged down in why or how you do this. Also remember that you are likely to be a bit raw here. You may think you owe someone an amends when you really don't. Consult with your support staff.

This level is about preparation. It is about making sure we are ready to move into one of the most powerful practices we can do to ensure happiness in our lives. This practice is called forgiveness, and while it is one of the most powerful, it is also one of the most difficult, and also the most rewarding. You will serve yourself well if you do some prep work here.

Remember that this isn't about THEM. It is about you. It isn't about excusing or condoning wrong or bad behavior on the part of others. It is about you being happy and free.

It is about continuing to change the way we think about what happened. When we look at this list, however you choose to create it, it is about saying good bye for once and for all the shackles that have kept you in victimhood for so long. It is also about taking responsibility for your life, which is about personal empowerment.

---

[6] Alcoholics Anonymous, www.aa.org

Chapter 9

9. Made direct amends to such people wherever possible, except when to do so would injure them or others.

Let's examine what amends means. It does not mean we apologize. Some of us have been apologizing our entire lives. It means very little unless followed by action. Amends means setting things right, and not repeating the action. It means saying, "I was dishonest, I lied to you. What can I do to set things right?"

In this level, we are setting right the behaviors we discovered in the fourth column.

I have consistently found this to be the most powerful thing I can do in my life to ensure happiness, peace and freedom. This step is the most difficult, and the most powerful. I think it is more difficult and powerful than 4 and 5. There is no mistake that there is a set of promises in the textbook of Alcoholics Anonymous that come immediately after fulfilling this step. I repeat those promises here:

"If we are painstaking about this phase of our development, we will be amazed before we are halfway through. We are going to know a new freedom and a new happiness. We will not regret the past nor wish to shut the door on it. We will comprehend the word serenity and we will know peace. No matter how far down the scale we have gone, we will see how our experience can benefit others. That feeling of uselessness and self-pity will disappear. We will lose interest in selfish things and gain interest in our fellows. Self-seeking will slip away. Our whole attitude and outlook upon life will change. Fear of people and of economic insecurity will leave us. We will intuitively know how to handle situations which used to baffle us."[7]

If you have done this work, you will discover that these promises indeed come true.

By the way, this is the power level. All that hullaballoo about powerlessness in the first step, the way it was originally written? Gone. We get megawatts of power here, and we keep that power if we continue the journey as it is described in the next three steps.

And here is another area where I see many people getting stuck. Having this much power in our lives is a bit scary at first. I remember the first time I realized I had all this power. It scared me to death. Because with power comes responsibility. In claiming the power I had to also claim responsibility. It meant I could no longer blame anyone or anything for my troubles. Regrettably, I see many people living in steps 1, 2 and 3 because they won't or can't claim their power. Don't do this. Claim your power. It really is a wonderful place to be.

Back to making amends.

This is another of those places where it is wise to consult with a member of your support staff. Sometimes we won't yet be capable of thinking clearly about a certain person or situation.

---

[7] http://www.aa.org/

We may be tempted to still blame them, or want to stay in the story a while. Or we may simply not know what to say to them, or how to say it.

You can do some role playing with your support staff.

There are some practical considerations here. Don't tell someone's spouse that you had relations with their significant other, especially if they are still together. You don't get to be selfish here. This is about clearing your side of the street, but not at the expense of someone else. If your amends will do someone else more harm than good, don't do it.

Amends are best made in person when possible. If that isn't possible, a phone call can work. If a phone call isn't possible, a letter will have to do.

Remember that what you are doing here is clearing your side of the street. You are clearing your clutter. The other person's response has nothing to do with you. This is about you and you only.

You may call them and ask for an appointment to see them and they might say no. That is their right to do. They are not under obligation to see you. You are taking time out of their lives to clear your side of the street. If they don't want to see you, so be it. If this happens, you then have a choice. You can write them a letter, explaining what you are attempting to do. You can apologize for your part, and ask what you can do to set things right. And thank them for their time. If they don't respond, you've done your part. Or you can simply let it go, knowing that you did the best you could, and be willing to make amends should the opportunity arise at a later date.

In my case, with the story of my ex, he lived about an hour or so away from me. And easy drive. I called him and asked to meet him. He asked why and I told him. We arranged a meeting in a public place, and I apologized and asked what I could do to set things right. Now remember he was the one who said horrible things to me upon leaving, he was the one who gave up on the marriage, he was the one who was incapable or unwilling to grow so that we could be more intimate. What was my part? My part was my behavior after the divorce. The anger, the attempts to manipulate our mutual friends into taking my side. I apologized for that, and said I would not be repeating that behavior. And I didn't. Not only did I not have to revisit what happened in our marriage, but I also did not have to repeat the behavior I did afterwards. There was a bonus to making amends to him: we became friends. That friendship lasted until he died. I still think fondly of him. I remember his strengths and the gifts he brought to my life and what our relationship taught me.

This is one of the most powerful things you can to do ensure freedom and happiness in your life.

Make amends one at a time, then let it go. You've done the work. You need not revisit the situation, you need not revisit any part of this. It is done. If for some reason you find yourself revisiting the situation, it means one of two things: either you haven't completely done the work, or there are deeper levels to visit which you could not access before. Repeat the process (steps 4-9) and experience all the healing and freedom life has to offer.

Chapter 10

10. Continued to practice self-reflection as a way of life, and remove the clutter as it happens.

The process described in levels 4-9 can be done over and over again. When you consistently and persistently change the focus from what THEY are doing or have done to your part, without shame or blame, and when you become aware of some clutter that you have allowed to accumulate and remove it, you will find that life becomes much more rewarding.

Life isn't about bad things happening to good people. It isn't about dealing with unpleasantness. It isn't about protecting ourselves. It isn't about doing to them before they do to you. It isn't about keeping up with the Joneses, nor is it about trying to get to that green grass on the other side.

It is about us, and how we feel about ourselves, and our actions, and who we be.

This is an ancient spiritual practice called introspection. It has served countless generations of people for eons, and it is recommended in every spiritual and non-spiritual path known to humankind. Self-awareness is key. When we are aware of who and what we are, we can then take responsibility for ourselves, and in that responsibility is power and peace.

This practice should continue for your lifetime. This is where you live. It isn't something to be done for a few minutes each day. It is a way to live. It is a lifestyle. It isn't about being so absorbed with self that you are of no earthly value to your fellows. It's about being aware of what you are thinking and feeling in relationship to your fellows and the events around you, so that you can act in accordance with your beliefs. Remember that your thoughts create your destiny. It is wise to know what those thoughts are. That is what this level is about. It really is a form of honesty. Honesty with yourself first, and then with the rest of the world. It is impossible to be honest with the rest of the world if you aren't first honest with yourself.

In terms of the analogy of cleaning the cupboards, it is about keeping on top of the clutter. Once having cleared the clutter, you will find that things have a way of creeping in. It is about paying attention, and continuing to clear away the clutter when necessary.

There are probably as many ways to do this as there are people. Some like to journal. Some like to do art. Personally, I will journal if it is something big that is confusing to me. But mostly, I just live this. There is a part of me that is always sort of watching me, noticing. Mostly I do it with humor and find myself saying, "really Karen....REALLY?!?" much of the time. But it really is a lifestyle, not something I do a few minutes each day and then let it go.

For those of you who really really really dislike the word powerless, which is in the original version of the 12 steps, this step and the previous one is where you get your power back. For most of us, we came to this way of life because life as we knew it sucked. Whether you call it powerless or unmanageable or just knew something had to change, most of us were unwilling to do this process unless there was some desperation involved. There does indeed seem as if there is an element of powerlessness when life is against us. Nothing seems to go our way, and things are falling apart everywhere we turn. Whether it is called powerlessness or something else, it does seem to indicate that a change is needed. If you have done the work up to this point, and continue to deepen and enlarge your spiritual life and your connection with a god of your understanding, you can be guaranteed that you will get power in your life.

And here I would like to say a few words about what having power means. Someone[8] once said that with great power comes great responsibility, and I believe that. When we get to this stage in life, this stage where we have cleaned much of our past, and are have a lifestyle of personal accountability and spirituality, we do get power. And with this comes responsibility. We have a responsibility to ourselves to no longer be victims, and to take care of ourselves. We have a responsibility to not blame anyone for anything. I don't know about you, but when I first realized this, it was like the proverbial burning bush. I had to stop and ask myself if I really wanted that much power. Fortunately for me and others, it was too late to go back to the old way of living. It was move forward or nothing, and I chose to move forward. Having power like this is scary, and I have found that many people, particularly in 12 step circles, don't want it. This is where you get to examine where you stand on the subject, for it is only you that can decide how much power you want in your life. Personally, I like having power!

---

8 Voltaire is commonly given credit for saying it first, although it is also attributed to many others

Chapter 11

11. Continued to enlarge and deepen and strengthen our connection with spirit.

This level is the most fun one for me. It is about study, it is about learning. For me, this isn't about jumping from one spiritual path to another in yet another attempt to get fixed or to find the answers. That is called being a spiritual athlete, and I don't know about you, but that just makes me tired.

Instead, this level is about enlarging my connection to and my concept of spirit. There are probably as many ways to do this as there are people. Personally, I prefer reading and discussion, coupled with meditation. I have spent the last 10 years of my life taking classes. Now I get to teach them. It's all the same stuff. I have found that what I most want to teach is what I most want to learn. And I am totally and completely and happily addicted to books. My favorite Christmas present last year was a stack of books almost two feet high, and a $100 gift card for Amazon.com.

But reading may not be for you. In this area where I live, the weather is mild and the scenery beautiful and many of my students do their spiritual work outside. They walk, they hike, they ride bikes, they ride horses. One lady I worked with talked about going outside in the middle of the night to watch the moon. I've been known to do some of that myself.

Again, this is about a lifestyle, not a thing you do once a day and then forget about it. Nor is it about something you do once a week (think going to church) and forget about. Consider the Buddhist practice of mindfulness. It is about being mindful of the presence of god stuff in everything you do and everywhere you go. It is about maintaining and enlarging a consciousness of spirit, in all your affairs, in everything you do during your days. If reading does it, do that regularly. If gardening does it, do that regularly. But consciousness is all of our being, and in conjunction with the introspection from step10, we develop a consciousness of god stuff that is beautiful to feel, 24/7.

Chapter 12

12. Having had a personality change as a result of doing this work, we now venture into the world of service, recognizing that serving others is a powerful way to live.

Before I get into the giving part, I want to say a bit about the personality change. I mentioned this before, in step 8. The appendix of the textbook of AA defines a spiritual awakening as a personality change. And it states that we will experience a "profound alteration in our reaction to life."[9] That was what happened to me, and if you have completed this work, it is happening to you also. This work changes us at the level where change is profound and permanent: inside of us. We can change who and what we are, and I believe that some of us needed to do so. I made that change, and so have you if you've done this process.

Now, about service.

The Centers for Spiritual Living have a vision statement: "Create a world that works for everyone."[10]

---

9 Alcoholics Anonymous, www.aa.org

10 www.csl.org

Setting aside the arguments of whether this can or should be done (as some people disagree with this statement), this step is about our giving back what we have received. Some call it the law of attraction, some call it the law of circulation. Some call it paying it forward. I call it life. It's a part of life, to give. It is a part of life to share who and what we are: our talents, our time and our treasure. It is not only about giving to receive, it is more about giving for the sheer joy of giving, because really, isn't that what life is all about?

We can't begin to approach this vision until we first create a world that works for ourselves. Hopefully you've made great strides in doing so by completing this process. Profound congratulations are in order! If you have reached this step, I think you should have a party. I think you should celebrate! When you are done with the party, come back and contemplate how it is you wish to serve.

Why serve? There are so many reasons. I'm reminded of Shakespeare's "let me count the ways in which I love you!"

Serving is fun, first of all. It is rewarding. And we get to decide how we wish to serve. We can give of our time, our talents, our treasure. I've done all three, and continue to do so. Giving of my time seems to be the most easy for me at this point. I currently look at my talents as things I worked hard to get, and feel I should be paid for them, so it's a bit difficult to give them away. I'm working on it, because I know the value of giving. I give of my treasure what I can, and have found that the 10% tithe suggestion works very well in terms of increasing my gratitude and flow of abundance.

The point is to give unselfishly of your time, talents or treasure. We don't get to specify how people use what we give them. The gift is because we want to give it. If you are giving with an expectation of control, you've just blocked all the yummy flow that can come from giving. Don't give a gift and then tell the recipient what you want done with it, or place conditions on the gift. This is about the law of circulation, or karma. It is about gratitude, which in reality is an ancient and powerful spiritual practice. Gratitude isn't simply about saying thank you. Gratitude is really an action, although it is also a state of being. But I believe that I get the feeling of gratitude by doing.

For example, if I am grateful for my health, then I am willing to eat right and exercise. Eating right and exercising is a way of increasing that for which I am grateful. In doing so, I then become even more grateful for having the time to exercise and the money to buy quality food. When I am aware of that gratitude, then I am aware of the business that continuously comes my way, bringing in funds that allow me to be more grateful for the business, and onward.

When I work with another person, or teach a class, and see the light come on in their eyes, I am grateful. When I give to an organization that does good in the world, I am grateful. When I tithe to a community that I love, I am grateful. And when I am grateful, I receive more of that for which I am grateful.

Do you see how rewarding service can be?

Conclusion

Once you have completed this process, I suggest you begin now to live in steps 10, 11 and 12. There is never any need to revisit steps 1, 2 and 3. Instead, I suggest you **become** the ideals embodied in steps 10, 11 and 12. Live them. It isn't so much about acting as it is being. Be those ideals and the right actions will come. And you will be free, and at peace.

After completing this process you should at least be able to say you are having moments where you feel like a pillar of peace. Keep this up and pretty soon the moments will expand in quantity and quality until you are one giant constant pillar of peace, no matter what happens in the world of conditions.

I'm not promising that life won't happen. I am not promising that discouragement and loss won't happen. But when it does, you won't react to it the same way, and you will still maintain that sense of peace and freedom.

Thank you for reading, and thank you most of all for doing this work.

Sincerely, Karen Linsley, M. A.

Appendix

What follows is a list of authors. I've not read every book these authors have written, but I've read at least one each, believe it or not. I provide this list as a jumping off point for you, dear reader. If you can find a bookstore, go browse in the self-help aisle, which is where most of these books live. Or look up the authors on your favorite online bookseller and see if something jumps out at you.

Some of these books I would classify as having to do with god stuff, some are purely self-help, and a few fall into the science category. There is some overlap with almost all of them, for these authors recognize a New Thought about ancient spiritual truths: the way to god is through yourself.

Here is the list, in no particular order:

Alcoholics Anonymous. Ok, so there is no author, officially, for this book. This book is known as the textbook of Alcoholics Anonymous.

Ernest Holmes
Neale Donald Walsh
Roger Teel
Edward Viljoen
Parker J. Palmer
Wayne Dyer
Chris Michaels
Louise Hay
Dennis Merritt Jones
Thich Nhat Hanh
Bryon Katie
Brene Brown

Deepak Chopra
Don Miguel Ruiz
Eckhart Tolle
Jeff Anderson
Gregory Toole
Carol Davis
Julia Cameron
Karen Russo
Mark Gilbert
Rocco Errico
Marcus Borg
Amit Goswami
Andrew Newberg and Mark Waldman

Enjoy the journey!

Made in the USA
Lexington, KY
23 September 2019